Walking With God

By
Julie Rezendez

Walking With God
Julie Rezendez

Published By Parables
September, 2020

All Rights Reserved. No part of this book may be reproduced or utilized in any form or by any means, electronic or mechanical, including photocopying, recording, or by any information storage and retrieval system, without permission in writing from the author.

    ISBN 978-1-951497-87-3
    Printed in the United States of America

Readers should be aware that Internet Web sites offered as citations and/or sources for further information may have been changed or disappeared between the time this was written and the time it is read.

Walking With God

By
Julie Rezendez

Table of Contents

Introduction
Four Categories of Prayer
Lectio Divina or Sacred Reading
Fasting
Sabbath Rest

Julie Rezendez

Introduction

Why do we need a book on spiritual disciplines? Christians have so many books on prayer already; don't they know how to pray? The answer to this question is yes and no. The problem lies in our excessive consumption of sensory overload. We seek to be handed every bit of information, rather than seeking to find it ourselves. We have forgotten how to slow down, how to listen, and how to connect with God. Some of this information serves as a reminder of who we are and who God is: the one true Lord, and manager of our lives.

Spiritual disciplines scare some of us into thinking that something difficult is required, an intense experience of fasting on bread and water or something equally rigid. Nothing could be further from the truth; these disciplines are easy to adapt and try. After all what does Jan Johnson say about fasting, "Fast what you can, not what you can't." This comes from a spiritual director, Jan Johnson, a leader in this field, one of those scholarly, Super-Christians, with many letters after her name. I have never experienced this attitude towards spiritual disciplines before; this is phenomenal. My experience as a child growing up scarred me for life on those fasting days. I was hypoglycemic, wanting to faint without any food, and sometimes later actually passing out. This is a prediabetic condition that plagues many of us. So complete fasting can make us feel horribly weak and sick. We need to understand alternative methods to traditional fasting that does not make us feel like passing out. After all, doesn't this defeat the purpose right from the start? Who are we trying to impress? God is displeased with pious religion, remember the Pharisees? Pharisees try to impress others by loud prayers in public or, by making a spectacle of their fasting, Matthew 6:16-18.

This book will include some important spiritual disciplines to help guide others to a deeper and more satisfying walk with God. Many Christians seek to know God better – these disciplines are a way that he is more easily accessible. Spiritual Disciplines help Christians align their lives with God's will, and to know just what his will is. This book is unique in that it contains a variety of disciplines instead of the usual type. Many books on spiritual disciplines offer one or two types at best, leaving many others out. This book will include four unique disciplines that are effective for spiritual growth, including four unique types of prayer disciplines which are very "User Friendly". Anyone can use these disciplines immediately, regardless of length of time being a Christian or seminary degree; they are simple and relevant. These disciplines are useful for the veteran Christian as well, bringing newness and a freshness to their Christian walk.

This book is a starting point towards growth – a guideline to a deeper level of relationship with God that satisfies our deepest longings and needs. Many Christians know that they have a gaping hole inside that only God can fill, but they do not know how to align themselves so he can fill it. Well here is a resource, a tool useful for that kind of growth.

I feel that this book is necessary to the church today because so many people leave church wanting more from God, and for themselves spiritually. This book will teach others how to find communion with God, and how to draw closer to Him. Many Christians rely on their church for spiritual formation which cannot meet the need in so short a span of time. We need to "Walk", this one out every day, in our day-to day existence, here are some tools necessary for that kind of growth. So, if you are seeking a closer walk with God, desiring to grow beyond the "Milk" bottle feedings to the "Meat" of knowing God deeply, then this book is for you. While it may seem very short and simple, it is the content that matters, not the sheer size of the volume.

Julie Rezendez

Four Categories of Prayer

This chapter will focus on four categories of prayer; Silence and Solitude, Beholding the Lord, Praying the Scriptures and Breath Prayers. Why do we need to learn all these different types of prayer? So we can have the ability to access them as needed, and to use each one at the appropriate time. During our quiet time with God, and with our difficult boss, our tough day, unexpected difficulties… We need to be able to adapt our structure of prayer based on our spiritual need at the time. After all, he is here to help, to offer us some comfort and peace of mind on this journey.

Silence and Solitude

Many of us see prayer as talk, talk, talk, when true devotion is shown through listening. We show God what we truly desire to experience from him by the level of real communication we give him. Our teaching in the past may have been only to express our needs to him, but we must not limit our communion with God to asking only. I am not saying that we will not express our needs and desires, but they will no longer control, or monopolize, our time with God. In Ecclesiastes 5:1-2 it reads, "Guard your steps when you go to the house of God. Go near to listen rather than to offer the sacrifice of fools, who do not know that they do wrong. Do not be quick with your mouth; do not be hasty in your heart to utter anything before God. God is in heaven and you are on earth, so let your words be few." We should be ready to listen, and eager to hear, not relying on man's wisdom but relying on God's infinite wisdom instead.

So many of us shy away from this discipline because at times it can be hard; the distractions lead us astray. However, if we are willing to acknowledge and push through our distractions, then we can come to be fulfilled by, and enjoy, this type of discipline. The difference being made in how we approach our times of silence, and how we prepare our hearts for it. I noticed that if I took along a short passage of scripture or some worship music on my phone, then it was easier to be silent afterwards. If I approached it with no help it became difficult and the distractions seemed to be very pronounced. I needed to experience his presence in some meaningful way before I would be able to listen carefully to him. This discipline gets easier over time, but especially at the outset I recommend something to help us focus our thoughts on him alone.

We clearly must not approach him with our agenda, thinking mistakenly that he will speak clearly about this or that, because he may or may not. Many times, we feel an intense sense of his love; the Holy Spirit just sits with us a while. No communication other than a reassurance of his love and care. We need to allow him to approach us in any way that he chooses and not with any idea beforehand, or else we are setting ourselves up for a bitter disappointment, thinking that God does not desire to speak to us. We cannot manipulate him into appearing as a "Genie from a bottle", simply because we are sitting silently before him. This discipline will challenge you, and the enemy of our souls will challenge it, because he controls you if he can distract you from spiritual matters. In other words, God is not found in the distractions, they take us away from him. Many distractions are good, for example: our families, our ministry, or our work. These distractions are ongoing and may make time alone with God difficult, however, we must prioritize our lives to include this time with Him.

      Naturally this discipline will look different for one person than it does for another, some prefer to walk, some hike, some are just off by themselves somewhere. Where you go does not matter it is the solitude that counts. We must truly be alone with him; this can be scary at times because it forces us to see ourselves and to embrace the areas that need changing. We must give in to this character growth, especially if we want to be transformed into his likeness. Many times, I am reminded of an un-confessed sin or something I should not have said – he will gently remind me of this. I will not be able to go on listening until I have dealt with this issue. If we try to avoid the correction, we will leave our time of solitude unfulfilled as if we missed something vital in this exchange. We must be pliable as clay to listen sincerely with our hearts. We can learn to be open-minded and to experience whatever he desires for us that day. If he points out our flaws it is for a reason, not to hurt us, but to help us see where we have strayed off the path he set before us. To help us grow in a certain area that we may not be able to see, or understand that we need the growth in.

      These next two types of prayer, both Beholding the Lord, and Praying the Scriptures, come from an ancient mystic, Madame Jeanne Guyon, of France. Here I have included two basic types of prayer from her book called, "Experiencing the Depths of

Jesus Christ"; Madam Jeanne Guyon also teaches different levels of spiritual growth beyond what we are discussing here. What does a seventeenth century Saint have to say to us currently about prayer? Well, has the bible message changed in any way? Of course not, neither has certain aspects of prayer, they have not changed, nor has our need for him changed; we still need to seek him out. The bible message is unique in that it contains a certain timeless aspect giving it both historical references in its time, and a timely relevance in our time as well. Many ancient mystics from the past have a very relevant message for us now especially in our busy, hectic lives. In fact, our looking back to the spiritual leaders of the past is a good concept because of our busy lives; they knew and practiced so many things that we have easily forgotten or discarded. In Beholding the Lord, Madam Guyon teaches us to bask in his presence, to peacefully and quietly rest in him. Begin by reading a short passage of scripture. It does not need to be overly long to serve this purpose: shorter is probably better. After you have read a passage of scripture, you will sense the Holy Spirit. The scripture has brought you into his presence, which is exactly the purpose to bring us closer to him. Now rest in his presence, the scripture has done its job, now we quietly listen, waiting on him, and what he might want to convey to us. I really appreciate the Lord's Prayer for this exercise, where we, his servants, agree to do his will here on earth, as he desires. I feel that this is very powerful supporting us in our service to him. We need to be able to wait on him, to quiet our minds, away from the distractions that pull us from our path that he has designed for us. This discipline, like many others disciplines, teaching us to rest in him, quietly waiting. We will need faith to believe that we are in his presence and that he will visit us there. Sometimes the hardest thing is to sit still, quietly waiting on him; it feels kind of lazy, as if we should be doing something else. Our industrial society teaches us to work, work, and work, not to quietly sit still. It is ingrained into our brains right from the start. If we want to draw close to him, we must be willing to sacrifice some of our time. We need to make room for him, as some might say to pencil him into our schedule, to open some time that is devoted to him, just to him, and developing our relationship with him. These disciplines will do just that, if we will practice them regularly, they will enhance our relationship with him greatly. Soon we will grow to the point that these types of discipline become habit, and we reach a whole new level of spiritual growth that we never thought possible.

  Our next lesson from Madam Guyon is; Praying the Scripture, this discipline is like an ancient practice called *Lectio Divina*, or sacred reading, but we will discuss that in detail later in this book. Praying the Scripture involves slowly mulling over a passage of scripture in your mind. To read the scripture listening for him to speak to us through it, not just for basic bible knowledge. This is not a time for reading for information, this is a quiet discipline designed to help us enter his presence through careful, slow reading of scripture, allowing God to speak to us within the context of the passage. When we sense what the Holy Spirit is saying in the passage, we can read it again even more slowly to truly absorb its meaning. When the words jump out at us, or we sense a profound lesson in a small part of a passage, that is the important part we must savor and discover for ourselves. Then this important part can become our prayer to him; we can repeat back what we have learned in prayer. This type of reading works well with short passages, part of a Psalm perhaps, or a portion of scripture. It is also helpful to hear something new in an old passage long since memorized; it can become new and alive again in this way. For example, John 3:16, "For God so loved, *so loved,* what does it mean to "So Love"? It means to love the world, every person, every nation, every face, to give your son that you also "So Love" and sacrifice him for all of us. If we look closely sometimes, we can see something different that we might have missed or rushed pass. This discipline is meant for our most quiet times, our resting, and waiting on him, our solitude. The word of God can become alive again and brand new if we are willing to quiet ourselves before him. Sometimes we may feel weak and undeserving of him and his presence, but he has called all believers into a relationship with him.

Another form of prayer that I learned from Dr. Jan Johnson, in her book, "When the Soul Listens", involves us quieting ourselves and our desires, replacing them with his. Dr. Johnson calls these "Breath Prayers", a simple prayer used to change our perspective towards his, especially at crucial, critical times. When dealing with a difficult person Dr. Johnson advises that we use this method. As we inhale, we can say, "More of Jesus", as we exhale, we can say "Less of me", (for example); this technique can be adapted to any circumstance needed. Here Dr. Johnson describes our using this method to deal with a difficult person. She reminds us that hurting people hurt people, so she tries to understand this person with the Lord's help. I love this exercise because it can be tailored to suit your own needs and circumstance that you find yourself in. Many Christians use a form of this type of prayer already; we are merely expanding on the premise and naming it. Sometimes we will say in our minds "Jesus please help me," because on our own we will say something that he might not want us to say. This method helps us to bite our tongue, when an inappropriate remark is coming to mind. This method applies to many situations; in my marriage, my employment, in all my relationships with others. Taking a step back and listening to God helps us to be better people, better friends, and better spouses; better all around. God is molding us to his image, and to the image of his son. This is merely a reminder to some of us, and a revelation to others; a lesson in maturity and humility.

      Now we are ready to explore the ancient practice of Lectio Divina, or "Sacred Reading". While this discipline is like the others, it has a specific method to it that is very helpful. We will briefly discuss some of the history behind the Lectio Divina practice before we explore the Lectio Divina Outline. Some dispute the authorship of the Lectio Divina exercise with another Monk named William of St. Thierry, but we will simplify our experience with the more popular authorship belonging to the Twelfth Century Monk named GuigoII. Do not be intimidated by the sense of his superior spirituality being a monk, we are all on the same path towards spiritual growth, just as he is. We must consider him as a teacher, a spiritual leader with something important to impart to us. GuigoII wrote a composition around the premise of Jacob's ladder in scripture. The Fool, (Us), use the ladder metaphorically to reach heaven through the
Lectio Divina exercise. The bottom rung on the ladder being Step one of the exercise or Read. Step two being the next rung on the ladder to Reflect or Meditatio, the next rung in succession being Step three Oratio, or to Respond and finally Step four being to Rest or Contemplatio, reaching heaven to experience his divine presence.

The beauty of this practice lies in its simplicity, and in the way it can be easily adapted by anyone. This practice does not replace any reading for general biblical knowledge, such as reading through the bible in a year; instead it is a companion to the basic knowledge premise. A spiritual discipline designed to allow us to experience God, and the Holy Spirit within the scriptures, in the context of a short biblical passage. In a quiet, slow, meditative way, this discipline should be experienced for an hour or two depending on the amount of time we are willing to invest. There are four basic steps involved in the Lectio Divina method of reading. Step one is called *Lectio* or Read, preferably out loud read through the passage once, spending a few moments in silence afterwards. Step two is called *Meditatio* or Reflect, read aloud a second time, pausing to reflect on the passage, paying careful attention to anything that catches our eye or, that jumps out at us. Step three is called *Oratio* or Respond, How is God speaking to us in this passage, are we challenged toward change by God, refreshed or renewed, or loved. Sometimes we are challenged to confess a sin or to apologize to someone. We must communicate honestly to God to be effective in our spiritual growth. Step Four is called *Contemplatio* or Rest. Finally, we spend some time in his presence, enjoying his communication with us. In any way that he chooses to speak to us, we must be open to it, even if it comes in the form of a rebuke. Again, 1. Read, 2. Reflect 3. Respond and 4. Rest, this method is very simple and yet quite satisfying spiritually. It is incredible when God speaks to us personally, the God of this whole world, and universe. I continually find it fascinating how he is mindful of us, and how much love, care and concern he gives to us, even when we are less than, or missing the mark he intended for us. We so often are more concerned with our agenda, rather than his. A popular phrase says, "Break my heart, for what breaks yours", well, his heart might be concerned with things that we do not even know about; things that our finite, carnal minds cannot even begin to fathom. How will we find out if we do not seek him earnestly? Possibly he sees people, or suffering, for example, differently than we do. From a higher, more enlightened perspective, a perspective we can only imagine unless we seek him and know him. We must be transformed, sanctified by him, in him, and through him. Too often we place the responsibility for our spiritual growth into the hands of the church. While the church can and does meet the need, it cannot cover all our spiritual life; we are responsible for most of it. We must be proactive, fighting for growth and change within ourselves. This type of transformation is not limited to those in formal ministry- it is for all Christians, every one of us. We need to know him intimately, in a deep sense of knowing beyond our five senses, to a deep spiritual level beyond what we can reach on our own.

      Now we are ready to examine the discipline of Fasting. It is important to discover what the bible teaches us about fasting. What did Jesus think about fasting and did he practice it regularly? We need to be on the same level scripturally that we are taught. If the bible says that we should be fasting, then we should be, end of discussion. However, fasting may look different from one individual to the next, but we will cover that aspect later. Biblically fasting is discussed in both the Old and New Testaments. In fact, the discipline of fasting is mentioned most often in the Old Testament. However, Jesus himself fasted and clearly he expected us to fast often as spelled out in the Gospel of Matthew 6:16-18. Jesus teaches us precisely what fasting should look like and how it should be done: "When you fast, do not look somber as the hypocrites do, for they disfigure their faces to show men they are fasting. I tell you the truth, they have received their reward in full. But when you fast, put oil on your head and wash your face, so that it will not be obvious to men that you are fasting, but only to your Father, who is unseen; and your Father, who sees what is done in secret, will reward you." Jesus says "When we fast" not if – his instruction is clear; we should be fasting regularly. Christians today either do not fast often enough, or they fast with wrong motives seeking their own way, or to change God's mind about something. We must be careful to examine our motives and proceed cautiously, considering what the Spirit wants for us, and not only what we desire for ourselves. This is mentioned in Romans when the Apostle Paul instructs us to walk in step with the Spirit rather than our carnal minds. Romans 8:5-8, says "Those who live according to the sinful nature have their minds set on what that nature desires; but those who live in accordance with the Spirit have their minds set on what the Spirit desires. The mind of sinful man is death, but the mind controlled by the Spirit is life and peace; the sinful mind is hostile to God. It does not submit to God's law, nor can it do so. Those controlled by the sinful nature cannot please God." Sometimes we want certain things for ourselves that may even be harmful or detrimental to us, and God withholds them lovingly, not because he has any intention of hurting us.

    A careful examination of fasting throughout scripture is necessary to discover historically the reasoning and purposes behind biblical fasting and how it was applied. If we only consider the New Testament and how fasting is discussed, we will miss out on all the historical information that God has left for us to learn from and understand. Fasting biblically has been used for different meanings and life experiences, which after careful examination will enrich and enhance our own fasting experiences.

In the Old Testament five categories emerge as noteworthy instances where God's people fasted. This list is not exhaustive, but it does help to gain insight into the former practices of fasting. I found the most interesting and important example of fasting relating to repentance, in Jonah 3:6-9. Jonah warns the King of Nineveh of God's coming wrath upon the city and he immediately removes his royal robes and covers himself with sackcloth and ashes. Of course, this was commonly done in those days whenever someone blasphemed God or they were in great distress. The king orders even the animals and livestock to fast along with all the people of Nineveh in the hope of receiving God's mercy and forgiveness. While many Christians may fast and repent, I have discovered this is not taught regularly in churches. Many times, we are taught to repent simply by not doing the bad things anymore. This is a lesson in futility when tempted by real snares and sinfulness. Not every temptation can merely be willed away on its own. If we fasted and repented, we might have the power to truly be overcomers, and not fall victim to deep rooted sin in our lives.

Each of these spiritual disciplines interacts with the others concerning our desire to communicate with God. In two separate instances God spoke to spiritual powerhouses while they were fasting and praying. In Deuteronomy 9:9, we learn of Moses fasting for forty days and forty nights on Mount Sinai; fasting preceded the Ten Commandments being given to Moses. This is an enormous victory, God still speaks to us today, and we need to be seeking his face through fasting and prayer. Again, in Daniel 9:3

we discover Daniel fasting and later communicating with God in a mighty way. The angel Gabriel again visits Daniel as before and he imparts wisdom to him about the future. It is not a coincidence that these "God moments" occurred during times of fasting.

      Fasting during mourning was quite common in the Old Testament. I have not heard of this connection to mourning before, nor have I practiced it myself, nor have I seen anyone else that uses it. However, it is mentioned many times in the Old Testament, in Nehemiah 1:3-4, Nehemiah learns of the breaking down of the wall of Jerusalem, and the burning of the city gates. Nehemiah in response wept, prayed, mourned and fasted after learning the fate of his beloved city and people. After the death of Saul and his son Jonathan, David and his army mourned, wept and fasted the whole day. Now a connection is shown through mourning and fasting, which can be beneficial to all mourners seeking God's comfort during a most difficult time. After discovering the atrocities done to Saul and his sons, 1 Samuel 31:13, the valiant men took down their bodies, burned them, buried their bones, and fasted for seven days. Personal distress and mourning warranted times of fasting in the Old Testament. In Psalm 35: 13, David recalls putting on sackcloth and humbling himself with fasting. David is very distressed at the abandonment he feels from his friends. The Prophet Joel calls for a "Holy Fast" in Joel 1:13-15; the Prophet asks that the priest fast and declare a fast for the condition of the Children of Israel. Again, in Joel 2:12-15, the Prophet begs the Children of Israel to return to God with their whole heart, with fasting, weeping and mourning. Here we see fasting and mourning in the need for repentance.

The Prophet Isaiah discusses how fasting should be and criticizes those that fast with hypocrisy and insincerity. In Isaiah 58:4-7, we see what fasting can do to deliver the truly bound and help those in poverty. The Prophet accuses those that fast without the fruit of the spirit and have wrong motives. We discover that fasting is meant to also deliver us and heal us from deep seated problems and social concerns. We are warned to not to expect to be heard if we refuse to change our actions when we are not fasting as well. The Prophet Jeremiah also discusses hypocrisy and how God will punish those that refuse to approach him in absolute sincerity and honesty. In Jeremiah 14:11-16 we discover the rebellion of the people and the false prophets telling lies. Although they fast it is all in vain. We must fast with right motives allowing God to convict us of any improper motives or selfish desires. Again, we see a similar problem in Zechariah 7, where God not allowing the old ways of fasting to occur because of a lack of repentance and sincerity reigns.

The final discipline to uncover is Sabbath Rest, which seems to be ignored by many Christians today. When God gave us the Ten Commandments, he intended for us to observe a Sabbath day once a week, a day consecrated unto the Lord. Why? Because he has asked us to, that's why; because he asked us to remember the day to keep it holy. God himself rested after creating the earth; there is significance in rest that we busy people do not fully embrace or understand. Many of you may be thinking that Jesus nullified "The Law", making it a part of the past and we are no longer bound or obligated to observe those countless commands and laws. However, we are still asked in the New Testament to "Enter God's Rest", as we will discover later. Understandably, many consider that a need to observe the Sabbath is outdated, an

Old Testament tradition, abandoned by the finishing work of the cross. Also, legalism is surrounding this practice in the Gospel accounts. We see the run-ins Jesus had with the Pharisees that tried in vain to trap him into their idea of "The Law", and its requirements. In Matthew 12:1-13, we see this incident and in Luke 13:15 we see it once again how they desperately tried to find some wrongdoing in Jesus through his healing and helping others on the Sabbath. Do we, as God's children still need that sense of rest for our souls? Yes we do. In Hebrews 4: 1-12, we see a command, and it is a command to "Enter His Rest", as God's people. These passages are a grippingly unavoidable reason to observe the Sabbath rest today, right here, right now. It is a grievance to God if we are disobedient to God's word and his ideal for our lives. If it's important to God, it is important to us. We are asked to see the sanctification in obedience rather than the legalism in the commands; God has asked us as his people to enter into his rest, for a spiritual purpose; a holy work of sanctification, which we simply cannot obtain on our own. Of course, the choice is ours. What we do with the time we are given is our choice, but are we really giving him our lives if we constantly dictate how those lives are spent? We will have to ask ourselves these questions, considering what scripture is directing us to. In Exodus 31:13, God promises his sanctification work to his children, through Sabbath observance. In the gospels we see a struggle involving Jesus' authority to heal, (work), on the Sabbath and the Pharisees accusing Jesus of breaking the (Law), namely the Law of Moses. These passages bring us to an interesting conclusion; many people try to persecute others, creating an atmosphere of legalism and restraint. This is not the type of rest God wants us to be involved in. We are not asked to refrain from working out of a sense of duty. Rather, we are invited to enter the rest of God, for spiritual renewal, transformation, sanctification, and refreshment.

      Now if you are in ministry and you work on Sunday obviously this cannot be your day of rest, but another day can be a day of rest as well. If more people observed a day of rest we would not have as much burn out, nor people in ministry that are so overtaxed, and stressed out by the weight of the problems that they are expected to carry. Even Pastor's in small congregations can be called upon often, and forced to overextend themselves at times, simply because of the need to wear many "hats" to keep the ministry running. A balance between work, ministry, and rest must be observed to recharge and replenish the spiritual needs of the individual.

Julie Rezendez

Notes

Introduction
1. In a lecture during an online course from Hope International University, Dr. Jan Johnson, Course Min 6310, Developing the Spiritual Disciplines, June 2010.

2. *New International Version Study Bible*, Zondervan, Grand Rapids Michigan, 1985, the exclusive scripture used throughout.

Chapter 1
Silence and Solitude
1. *When the Soul Listens: Finding Rest and Direction Through Contemplative Prayer* by Dr. Jan Johnson, Nav Press Publishers, Colorado Springs Colorado. 1999. Pgs. 79-87.

2. MIN 6214 Spiritual Disciplines: Silence and Solitude, an online course, Dr. Alan Fadling, Hope International University, August 2011.

3. Min 6310, Developing the Spiritual Disciplines. An online course from Hope International University, Dr. Jan Johnson, June 2010. Beholding the Lord, Praying the Scriptures.

4. *Experiencing the Depths of Jesus Christ*, Madame Jeanne Guyon, Seed Sowers Publishers, Jacksonville, Florida. 1975. Breath Prayers

5. *When the Soul Listens: Finding Rest and Direction Through Contemplative Prayer* by Dr. Jan Johnson, Nav Press Publishers, Colorado Springs Colorado. 1999. Pgs. 15-27.

Notes

Chapter 2
Lectio Divina
1. John Green, Article the Golden Epistle and the Ladder of Monks: Lectio Divina in   the Context of the Twelfth Century Carthusian Spirituality. The Australasian Catholic Record, April 20, 2010, 215-228. Darling Library Hope International University retrieved online March 2012.

2. THE 5450 Lectio Divina: Reading the Classics, Online course, Hope International University, Dr. David Timms, August 2009.

3. MIN 6214 Spiritual Disciplines: Silence and Solitude. An online course, Dr. Alan Fadling, Hope International University, August 2011.

4. *When the Soul Listens: Finding Rest and Direction Through Contemplative Prayer* by Dr. Jan Johnson, Nav Press Publishers, Colorado Springs Colorado. 1999. Pg. 55.

Chapter 3
Fasting
1. Lynne M. Baab, *Fasting: Spiritual Freedom Beyond our Appetites*, InterVarsity Press, Downers Grove Illinois, 2006, P.13.

2. WWW. BibleGateway.com, website, March 2012.

3. *New International Version Study Bible*, Zondervan, Grand Rapids Michigan, 1985, the exclusive scripture used throughout.

4. Dictionary of Jesus and then Gospels, Article, InterVarsity Press, Downers 1992, Editors, Joel B. Green, Scott McKnight.

Chapter 4
Sabbath Rest
1. Lynne M. Baab, *Sabbath Keeping, Finding Freedom in the Rhythms of Rest*, 2005, InterVarsity Press, Downers Grove Illinois, 2006, P.13.

2. *New International Version Study Bible*, Zondervan, Grand Rapids Michigan, 1985, the exclusive scripture used throughout.

3. WWW. BibleGateway.com, website, March 2012.

Julie Rezendez

Suggestions for Further Reading

Devotional Classics: Selected Readings for Individuals and Groups, A Renovare Resource For Spiritual Renewal, Edited by Richard J. Foster and Bryan James Smith, Harper Collins Publishers, 2005.

Celebration of Discipline: The Path to Spiritual Growth, Richard J. Foster, Harper Collins Publishers, 1998.

Ruthless Trust: A Ragamuffins Path to God, Brennan Manning, Harper Collins Publishers, 2000.

Here and Now: Living in the Spirit, Henri J. M. Nouwen, Crossroads publishing, 1994.

In the Name of Jesus: Reflections on Christian Leadership, Henri J. M. Nouwen, Crossroads Publishing, 1984.

The Way of the Heart: The Spirituality of the Desert Fathers and Mothers, Henri J. M. Nouwen, Crossroads Publishing, 1981.

Soul Feast An Invitation to the Christian Spiritual Life, Marjorie J. Thompson, Westminster John Knox Press, Louisville Kentucky, 2005.

Living the Lord's Prayer, Dr. David Timms, Bethany House Publishers, Minneapolis, Minnesota, 2008.

Hearing God: Developing a Conversational Relationship with God, Dallas Willard, InterVarsity Press, InterVarsity Press, Downers Grove Illinois, 1999.

Julie Rezendez

www.ingramcontent.com/pod-product-compliance
Lightning Source LLC
Chambersburg PA
CBHW030203100526
44592CB00009B/420